Peter Wotschke

Electro-Planning

Peter Wotschke

Electro-Planning

BIRKHÄUSER
BASEL

Contents

Foreword

Electrical engineering is a specialized area of building services that in many projects is supervised by specialized planners. Architects are often responsible for coordination and communication with the client, and have to clarify the user and comfort requirements. Therefore, it is important that architects are familiar with the contents and options of electrical planning in order to integrate them into their designs from the outset and to address the complex requirements of users and functions.

While previously the electrical installation of a building consisted primarily of the supply of electricity and light via wiring, sockets, and switches, nowadays complex network components and intelligent building control systems form the basis of electrical installations. These include various structural components such as windows and doors, as well as building automation providing light, ventilation, and heating via additional controlled automation. The complexity of electrical installations in buildings has increased exponentially, not least due to the steady increase in user requirements and energy-saving objectives. Thus, electrical planning has become an integral part of any design and planning process.

Within this context, electrical engineering in recent years has gone from playing a rather subordinate role to becoming a central design issue. In order to be able to incorporate the guiding principles in the design and to optimize the interface with other specialist areas right from the beginning, comprehensive knowledge of the requirements and possibilities of electrical planning is imperative. In addition to the technical systems, this includes primarily an understanding of the networks and the range of installations used. *Basics Electro-Planning* provides a clear and comprehensive introduction to electrical planning for architects.

Bert Bielefeld, Editor

Introduction

With the advance of technical possibilities, the demands that contractors place on modern buildings are growing. Installation and operational functioning have to be carried out with a high degree of safety and great flexibility over the entire life cycle. Household functions are increasingly operated, monitored, and controlled electrically. At the same time, buildings are expected to have a low environmental impact and, above all, energy consumption should be kept to a minimum. Therefore, energy optimization is the most important measure for reducing the environmental impact of buildings.

For the architect, this means being informed about functional methods and technical developments in order to be able to implement the technical requirements of the contractors.

A particular challenge is the coordination of domestic engineering trades. The most important of these are: heating, air conditioning, fire protection, burglar protection, building control technology, and electricity distribution. The requirements cannot simply be divided among the individual trades but must be planned in a coordinated manner. A decisive factor is the networking of the components in electrical planning.

This volume provides an introduction to the planning of electro-technical installations and covers heavy current distribution and low current distribution, through to building control technology, in order to help architects attain a basic understanding of how they are all connected.

Basics of Power Supply

The standard power supply for residential buildings is usually pro- Voltage networks
vided by a 230 / 400 V low-voltage network. The medium-voltage network
(10,000 V or 20,000 V) supplies larger facilities, such as hospitals, administrative buildings, and department stores, while high-voltage networks (110,000 V) supply industrial plants.

In the case of electricity, depending on the current intensity and the Types of power supply
direction of flow, one can differentiate between various current types,
for example:

— Direct current: current and direction of the current flow do not
  change over time. Solar cells and batteries supply direct current,
  which is required for the operation of electronic devices.
— Alternating current: can change direction periodically. In Germany,
  almost the entire electrical power supply is based on alternating
  current. Plug sockets have alternating current and the majority of
  household appliances are operated in this manner.
— Three-phase current: combines several phase-shifted alternating
  currents. Households are supplied with three-phase current. Devices with higher power are usually connected via a three-phase
  current socket or directly, without an electrical outlet, for example
  an electric heater.
— Mixed current: direct current combined with alternating current

Furthermore, one can distinguish between different types of electricity, such as gray electricity from various electrical sources and green
electricity from renewable sources. The production of green electricity
is based on renewable biomass raw materials and sources, such as geo-
thermal energy, sun, and wind.

The power supply can be subdivided into two areas according to its High- and low-voltage electrical currents
use: the supply of a strong current of electricity mainly for the connec-
tion of electrical devices via sockets, and the provision of low-level current for the operation of information and communication devices with
which the operation of the building can be carefully monitored and controlled.

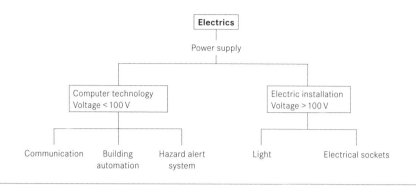

Fig. 1: Electrical technology in buildings

HIGH-VOLTAGE CURRENT EN ROUTE TO THE CONSUMER

The term "high-voltage current" is used for three-phase, alternating current. This principle is based on three interconnected, alternating currents, which enable the transport of electricity to the network. In order to be able to transport electricity, a certain amount of voltage is required.

If long distances need to be covered, then high or even maximum voltage is used. Due to its efficiency, it enables the transport of energy into regional or area-dependent networks.

High-voltage or three-phase current is thus required for the transport and subsequent distribution of energy. High-voltage current passes through various transformation processes before it ends up being used in households at a voltage of 230 V or 400 V. Voltages up to a maximum of 1,000 V are referred to as low voltage. Most electrical appliances in households, businesses, and industrial applications function with low-voltage current.

Technically speaking, a generator with three coils, arranged in a circle, is assembled for the generation of high-voltage current – hence the term "three-phase alternating current." This results in three alternating voltages, which can be employed at different times, thereby increasing performance.

This allows transport over long distances and the subsequent use – for example from the power station as a power generator – by the final consumer. > Fig. 2

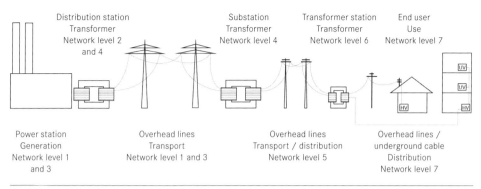

Fig. 2: Overview of a high-voltage network

Tab. 1: Grid-level structure in the network system of European electricity grid operators

Network level	Description	Classification	Voltage	Examples
NE 1	Transregional transmission network	High-voltage network	220/380 kV	Large power plants, wind parks, European network
NE 2	Distribution/substation	High to maximum voltage		
NE 3	District distribution network	High voltage	110 kV	Medium-sized power plants, e.g., bio and hydropower plants
NE 4	Distribution/substation	High to medium voltage HS/MS		
NE 5	Regional distribution network	Medium voltage	10/20/30 kV	Small power plants, e.g., wind, power, and photovoltaic systems
NE 6	Transformer station	Medium to low voltage MS/NS		
NE 7	Local low-voltage network	Low voltage	230 V/400 V	Small power plants, e.g., photovoltaic systems and fuel cells

In addition to high-voltage power plants, there are other voltage systems for energy transport. A heavy current system includes networks with a voltage of more than 50 V and currents of more than 2 A.

A high-voltage system can be divided into different voltage levels.
> Tab. 1

Depending on the power demand and the distance over which the power has to be transmitted, the appropriate voltage level is selected in order to minimize the loss of electrical energy from the power plant to the consumer. As a rule of thumb, it can be assumed that the maximum distance in kilometers is approximately the voltage in kilovolts. The alteration of voltage levels is achieved with the help of transformers in substations and, with smaller voltages, in transformer stations.

HIGH- AND MEDIUM-VOLTAGE SYSTEMS

For high- and medium-voltage networks, the primary components are the switchgear and the transformers. If large buildings or industrial plants are supplied with high-voltage current, this has to be integrated into the planning.

Switchgear can be described as the sum of all the components that are contained in control cabinets within a switchgear cabinet. In addition to various other components, control cabinets consist mainly of individual switchgear. Switching devices are devices for connecting (switching on) or interrupting (switching off) circuits, in order to disconnect them from the mains, or to ground them for short-term work. Switchgear for high- and medium-voltage networks is generally placed in its own room or container, where various safety regulations have to be observed.

Transformers are one of the most important components for energy transmission and distribution. With the help of transformers, voltages can be increased or decreased. A transformer consists of an iron core that connects two coils (primary and secondary coil). If an alternating voltage is applied to the primary coil, this causes an alternating current, which in turn causes a changing magnetic field in both coils.

Depending on the number of turns in the respective coils, the magnetic field induces a secondary voltage in the secondary coil, which is increased or reduced relative to the primary voltage. Their layout depends on the application, the construction, the rated power, and the transmission ratio.

The changing magnetic field also causes induction currents in the iron core. These heat the core, resulting in a loss of energy and the necessity to cool. This cooling can be carried out in liquid or dry form. Accordingly, transformers are differentiated into oil-filled, alternating transformers (oil transformers) and alternating-phase, dry transformers (GEAFOL transformers).

In oil transformers, electrical insulation and cooling takes place via mineral or synthetic oils. > Fig. 3 The use of such substances requires special planning measures for flooding and fire protection. For example, watertight collection tanks and collecting pits should be provided. Furthermore, rooms should be separated with fireproof walls and should have fire-resistant doors. Tanks and collection pits should be arranged to prevent the spread of fire.

In dry transformers, electrical insulation is provided via substances such as epoxy resins or by solid insulating materials. Cooling is carried

Switchgear

Transformers

Oil transformers

Dry transformers

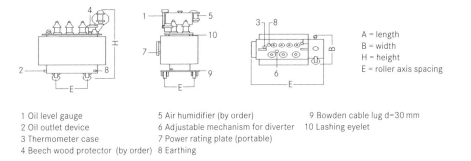

		A = length
		B = width
		H = height
		E = roller axis spacing

1 Oil level gauge
2 Oil outlet device
3 Thermometer case
4 Beech wood protector (by order)

5 Air humidifier (by order)
6 Adjustable mechanism for diverter
7 Power rating plate (portable)
8 Earthing

9 Bowden cable lug d=30 mm
10 Lashing eyelet

Fig. 3: Components of a transformer

out via convection in the ambient air, which ought to be taken into account when planning. Cast-resin transformers have an advantage over oil transformers, as the absence of an oil transformer eliminates the associated fire and groundwater risk. Moreover, they are nearly maintenance free and can be transported relatively easily. However, their use is limited to a power range of around 40 megavolt amperes (MVA) and an operating voltage of no more than 36 kilovolts (kV). > Fig. 4 ○

If transformers are housed in buildings, the design of the building must ensure that the transformers can be replaced. This involves correspondingly large external doors, access routes, and, if necessary, the ability for the transformers to be removed from the building on rails.

○ **Note**: Oil transformers are used as power transformers, for instance, in power supply systems, in transmission and distribution networks, in refineries, and on onshore and offshore platforms.

○ **Note**: Resin transformers are mainly used as distribution transformers in medium-voltage networks in the oil and gas industry, in foundries, aluminum production, and steelworks, as well as in public and commercial buildings such as airports, hospitals, etc.

Fig. 4: Example of a 40 MVA transformer

Fig. 5: Example of low-voltage switchgear

LOW-VOLTAGE SWITCHGEAR

Additional switchgear is required to supply low-voltage systems. Low-voltage switchgear and distribution boards provide the connections between equipment for generating (generators), transporting (cables, lines), and transforming electrical energy, on the one hand, and equipment such as heating, lighting, air conditioning, and information technology on the other hand.

As with medium-voltage switchgear, low-voltage switchgear is rarely built locally, but is rather delivered as ready-to-use switchgear. Most modular cabinet sizes are accommodated in separate switching rooms. > Fig. 5 It is sensible to schedule control-room floors as elevated floor systems, on which the control cabinets can be installed and below which the wiring supply can connect. > Fig. 6

Reactive-current compensation

Reactive-current compensation systems are of particular importance within the switchgear. Reactive current is a by-product of energy supply. It is the current required for supporting inductive loads (e.g., motors, transformers, ballasts, coils of any layout) necessary to produce a magnetic field. By means of reactive current, additional losses are generated in cables and transformers. Reactive current thus requires larger cable cross-sections, resulting in higher levels of energy loss during transmission. Therefore, in most industrial, commercial, and service industries – in addition to active energy – reactive current is also measured.

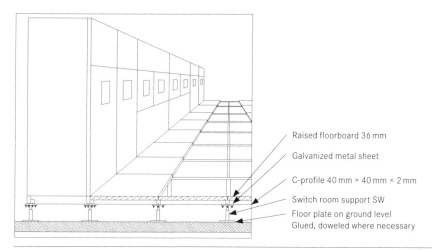

Raised floorboard 36 mm

Galvanized metal sheet

C-profile 40 mm × 40 mm × 2 mm

Switch room support SW

Floor plate on ground level
Glued, doweled where necessary

Fig. 6: Switchgear floor (Source: SYSBOTEC GmbH & Co. KG)

Reactive-current compensation systems can compensate for the generated reactive current by automatically adapting the necessary condenser
capacity to reflect the current demand.

GROUNDING CONDITIONS

Central high-voltage and low-voltage systems require grounding to
divert current flows into the earth. Depending on the grounding conditions of the current source, the kind of installation, the implementation
of the neutral conductor, and the safety conductor, the kind of power supply is differentiated into TN, TT, and IT systems. > Tab. 2

In this internationally consistent classification, the first letter indi-
cates the grounding conditions of the current source (T: direct grounding of the current source (operating earth); I: isolation of all active parts
in relation to earth).

The second letter classifies the grounding conditions of the operating installations and equipment (T: directly earthed body, independent of
an existing grounding; N: bodies connected directly to the earth source
of the current).

The basic network forms are derived from this, as summarized in
Tab. 2.

Network configuration	Power source	Body
TN System	Directly earthed	Grounded to the power source
TN-S		N and PE separately routed
TN-C		N and PE in one conductor
TN-C-S		N and PE partly combined, partly separated
		Neutral conductor (N) / Safety conductor (PE)
TT System	Directly earthed	Directly earthed
IT System	Isolated against earth	Directly earthed

Despite being hazardous in some instances, TN-C systems were frequently installed in households right up to the twentieth century. Nowadays, they are rarely used. TN-S systems, which are considerably more secure than the TN-C system, are mainly used in larger commercial plants. The TN-C-S system usually comprises a combination of a TN-C system, for example for the distribution network of the power supply, and a TN-S system in the customer installation.

The TT system is used as a standard in many European countries. IT systems, however, are mainly used in operating rooms of hospitals, in the chemical industry, or in the power supply of groundwater storage pumps.

The nature of the earth connection of medium- or low-voltage networks ought to be selected carefully, since it determines expenditure for safety measures. Furthermore, it also influences electromagnetic compatibility (EMC). Experience has shown that TN-S systems have the highest cost-benefit ratio for low-voltage electrical networks. > Chapter Elements of Low-Voltage Installations in Buildings, Earthing Systems

Types of Power Supply

In principle, power supply can be divided into four areas. The first two are responsible for the power supply of buildings.

— Public power supply: bulk of the electricity supply
— Private power generation: the largest group in numbers, but consumes the smallest share of total electricity generation
— Industry's own power plants
— Private systems, e.g., German Railways

Private power generators are relevant for the planning of buildings. Typical options are described in the following section.

PRIVATELY GENERATED ELECTRICITY

Privately generated electricity is fed into the public grid from wind-power plants, photovoltaic arrays, micro-hydropower plants, cogeneration plants (combined heat and power), and other small-scale power plants. This group, which is the largest in terms of numbers, nevertheless has the lowest share of total electricity generation. Direct photovoltaic (PV) and cogeneration (CHP) have primarily been used for direct electricity generation in buildings.

As a rule, private systems are connected to the public network in order for excess energy to be fed into the grid. However, electricity produced by private installations can also be used directly in the house without being connected to the public network. Such self-sufficient, network-independent systems (island systems) are common in remote buildings, such as mountain huts, where the effort or the costs associated with a network connection are prohibitive. The generation of power for direct consumption in buildings quickly reaches limits for regenerative sources (sun and wind), as energy sources are not continuously available in the required quantity, for example on windless or overcast days.

Connection to the public network

The demand for electrical energy is usually at its peak during times when the solar-based electricity generation yield is at its lowest. This applies, for example, to artificial light, when natural daylight is insufficient. Therefore, recovered energy must first be stored.

Storage of renewable electricity

The decentralized storage of renewable-generated energy still poses a particular technical challenge. Battery systems are usually space-, cost-, and maintenance-intensive, with short storage and discharge times. Therefore, batteries, rather than the public power supply network, are typically used as the storage medium. Thus, excess current is fed into the grid via a feed meter from the grid-fed inverter. This process is referred to as a network-coupled system.

Feed-in compensation The energy input is remunerated. The remuneration amount is stipulated by law, thus encouraging the consumer. As with all other consumers of electricity, homeowners draw the required electricity from the grid via a reference meter. The consumed quantity can be charged according to the amount of fed current. Thus, as a rule, the owners of privately owned installations do not use the self-generated energy themselves.

For each individual case, it has to be ascertained whether, or under which conditions, the use of private plants is economically justifiable and ecologically sensible. The most common installations used are photovoltaic plants and combined heat and power plants, which are described below.

PHOTOVOLTAIC SYSTEMS

Photovoltaic (PV) is the direct conversion of sunlight into electricity using solar cells, based on the so-called photoelectric effect. Light and negative charge carriers are released by light radiation in a semiconducting material (solar cell), thus generating a current flow in a closed circuit.

Since the resulting direct current cannot be used directly in households, it first has to be converted into alternating current by means of an inverter. The generated alternating current can then be consumed directly in the house or fed into the public grid. PV systems are fitted with shutdown and protective devices – against lightning strikes, for example.

The solar cells are interconnected with solar modules or solar panels, which are usually mounted on south-oriented roofs (in the northern hemisphere), integrated into the facade of buildings, or mounted on an open site. All solar modules are connected to one another to form the solar generator.

Solar modules or panels are available in various forms. In addition to the classic roof-mounted cells > Fig. 7, solar cells can also be incorporated into facade materials, roofing tiles, skylights, glass panes, and so on, thus providing scope for various architectural designs. In planning, however, optimal orientation should be considered in order to maximize efficiency. In addition, surfaces have to be cleaned regularly, in order to avoid any loss of efficiency due to the accumulation of dirt. When considering the life cycle of a building, it should also be noted that solar cells lose their efficiency over time, so that the possibility of replacement should be ensured.

Fig. 7: Installation of an array of roof-mounted photovoltaic panels (left) or as a building-integrated system (right)

COMBINED HEAT AND POWER PLANTS

The simultaneous production of electricity and heat in a single unit, which is mostly operated by gas, is referred to as a combined heat and power unit, or combined heat and power (CHP). In the plant, a gas combustion engine drives a generator that provides electrical power. The heat generated during this process is also used for heating and hot water treatment. CHPs achieve a high degree of efficiency through the double use of energy.

Depending on the application area, CHPs can be divided into different performance groups. For example, Maxi-CHPs are used for schools or administrative buildings, Midi-CHPs for small companies, Micro-CHPs for multifamily homes, and Pico-CHPs for single-family homes.

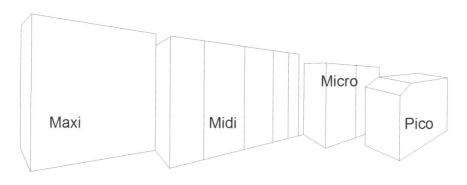

Fig. 8: Examples of combined heat and power plants (Source: ATN Hölzel GmbH)

This technology is mostly used in rural regions, or in urban housing schemes. The heat produced during the generation of electricity is used directly for heat supply in the vicinity of its production. As transmission losses are largely eliminated, CHP plants are thus able to achieve excellent efficiency levels of up to 92% – considerably higher than in the majority of large modern power plants, which have an efficiency of just over 60%. However, combined heat and power plants incur high maintenance costs.

Environmentally friendly combined heat and power plants have established themselves over the past few years, but due to their size, thus far they have predominantly been used for multifamily houses and commercial businesses. Economically viable plants suitable for single- and double-family houses, so-called Micro-CHP plants, have been on the market for only a few years. Like photovoltaic plants, combined heat and
■ power plants are being actively promoted.

■ **Tip**: If a replacement power supply system is being planned, it is imperative to check whether a combined heat and power plant would be economically viable with regard to the overall energy concept. An investment is generally worthwhile if the repayment period does not exceed seven years or, in justified cases, ten years.

PROTECTION OF THE POWER SUPPLY

Electric power can be supplied to buildings in various ways. Typically, three possible network structures can be distinguished:

1. The general power supply (AC) is the basic supply for all regular consumers.
2. The safety power supply (SV) supplements the AV supply and is intended to offer protection for the public, powering fire detectors or escape route lights in the event of a power failure or an emergency.
3. The uninterruptible power supply (UPS) supplies installations that have to be operated continuously even in the event of a power failure. These include, for example, electrical equipment in operating rooms, production machines in industry, or runway and tunnel lighting. The supply is then carried out via battery systems or emergency, diesel-powered units.

Generally, residential buildings only have one AC. A safety power supply is primarily used for large or public buildings.

A UPS system is required if the power supply has to remain uninterrupted for a maximum of thirty minutes even if, for example, the public power supply fails. One differentiates between a dynamic and a static UPS system. A risk analysis has to be undertaken as a basis for the planning of a UPS.

The two main components of a dynamic UPS are the electric motor and the generator, which are coordinated with each other as a machine set. Critical loads are supplied by the generator.
Dynamic UPS

Through the use of flywheel storage accumulators and/or battery systems, voltage drops can be bridged for a limited amount of time, usually in the range of seconds or minutes. Bridging time can also be extended by coupling a diesel engine; however, the accumulators must supply the generator with energy until the diesel engine is running.

In static UPS, components of power electronics such as diodes and transistors are used to influence the supply voltage. Static UPS systems are classified according to the job, the quality of the UPS output voltage, and the performance in the event of power failure:
Static UPS

- Classification 3: passive standby mode (off-line) as compensation for short-term mains failures, voltage fluctuations, and voltage spikes
- Classification 2: line-interactive operation as compensation for continuous low or excessive voltage
- Classification 1: double conversion operation (on-line), used, among other things, as compensation for short voltage surges, impact of sporadic lightning, and periodic voltage distortions

As a rule, larger UPS power units are used if spatial separation of electrical loads from the components of the electrical power supply is required.

For reasons of ventilation, electromagnetic compatibility (EMC), noise, maintenance, fire protection, and so on, the UPS and battery systems should be placed in discrete spaces.

Emergency power supply system (EPSS) If the power supply must be maintained without interruption for more than thirty minutes, an emergency power supply system (EPSS) has to be installed, which can generate electricity over a longer period of time. An emergency power supply must be drawn up to take the utilization factor into account only for those consumers for whom it is imperative to have uninterrupted power. Emergency systems should be planned where extremely important plants must be supplied with electricity.

Parallel UPS systems can be used to increase performance and improve availability. It should be noted, however, that as the number of components increases, so the service effort is increased. The system's increased complexity can in turn create new possibilities for error.

Tab. 3: Comparison of energy sources

Power sources	Transformer	Generator	UPS
Selection	Number and power according to the required power for a normal power supply	Number and power corresponding to the total power of the supplied loads if the transformers cannot supply energy	Number, power, and energy depending on the time required to provide an independent power supply and the total power of all consumers powered by UPS
Requirement	— High security of supply — Overload capacity — Low power dissipation — Low noise level — No restrictions for installation — Compliance with environmental, climate, and fire protection regulations	— Cover the energy for the replacement power supply — In turbocharger engines, take over the load in phases — Availability of sufficient short-circuit capacity to ensure shutdown conditions	— Stable output voltage — Availability of sufficient short-circuit capacity to ensure shutdown conditions — Low-maintenance buffer batteries for power supply — Compliance with noise level limits — Low harmonic load for the prearranged mains
Advantages	— High transmission capacity — Stable short-circuit currents — Electrical isolation	— Decentralized availability — Self-sufficient energy generation	— Low losses — Voltage stability — Electrical isolation
Disadvantages	— High current surges — Dependency on the public network	— Network instability in network fluctuations — Small, short-circuit currents	— Very low short-circuit currents

Elements of Low-Voltage Installations in Buildings

In order to use and distribute electricity in buildings, many components are necessary to achieve a complete electrical installation. In addition to the components of low-voltage installations presented in this chapter, low-voltage systems (such as for telephone and data technology) and, increasingly, building installations for building automation are also required, as is explained in the following chapters.

RESIDENTIAL CONNECTION

Residential connections to houses link the public network with an individual building. For this purpose, a mains connection is established in the public area, which is routed via a house connection line through the house entrance to the connection box in the house. Generally, standardized components are used, which route the cables in a watertight manner into basement outer walls or floor slabs and, if necessary, are connected with further connection lines. > Fig. 9

House connection box and distribution

Residential connections terminate in a house connection box, which is the interface between the power supply and private electricity distribution within the house. Furthermore, a central electricity meter or current counter is installed in the main distributor for each unit, in order to charge the consumers according to their consumption. Fuses and switches for the further utilization units or circuit distributors are located in the mains distributor. > Fig. 10 and Chapter Electrical Circuits

Residential installation room

Depending on the size and type of the project, different rooms for household connections and installations are provided according to local regulations. In smaller residential buildings, a combined space is generally possible for all installations. > Fig. 11 In principle, the layout of the wall surfaces should be planned so that all installations are accessible.

The dimensions of the floor areas in technical rooms are determined by the dimensions of the required components and the corresponding safety regulations. > Fig. 12 Additional aspects, such as room ventilation, ceiling loads, and circulation routes, must also be taken into account when planning technical spaces and buildings. Oversized spaces will reduce the building's profitability, while undersized spaces can lead to a facility being refused council approval, or else create the necessity for expensive custom-made solutions in order for the system to be able to function.

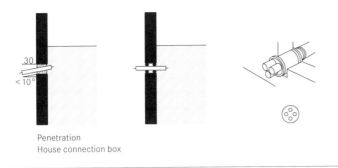

Penetration
House connection box

Fig. 9: Details of residential connections

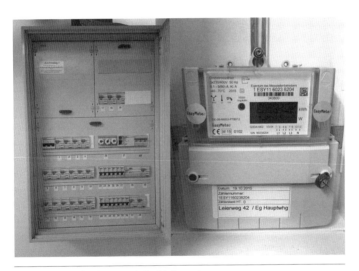

Fig. 10: Distribution boxes and electricity meters

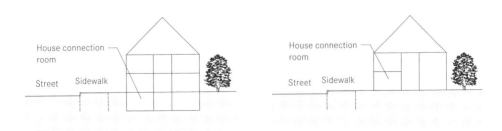

House connection room

Street   Sidewalk

House connection room

Street   Sidewalk

Fig. 11: Positioning of the residential connection room in the building

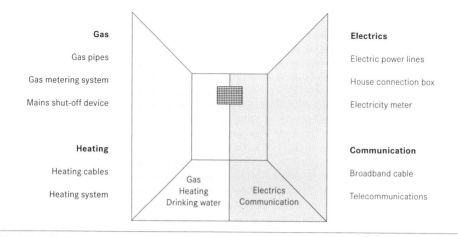

Gas	Electrics
Gas pipes	Electric power lines
Gas metering system	House connection box
Mains shut-off device	Electricity meter
Heating	**Communication**
Heating cables	Broadband cable
Heating system	Telecommunications

Gas
Heating
Drinking water

Electrics
Communication

Fig. 12: Installation principle of residential connections

EARTHING SYSTEMS

So-called "protective earthing" (PE) is an indispensable part of the power supply of buildings. PE provides protection against electric shock and lightning. Earthing provides for the conduction of electrical voltages or different potential energy (e.g., lightning strikes). Earthing systems must be connected to the potential equalization.

Ground (earth) rods, rings, and foundation earth electrodes can be used for grounding.

Ground / earth rods   A ground rod is generally perpendicular to the ground and inserted deep into the ground. The earth depth is the simplest solution for retrofitting a grounding or lightning protection system. A depth of 9 m is recommended. If several ground rods are used, then the required earthing depths can be divided into several parallel lengths. All ground rods have to be connected with a ringer.

Ring ground   A ring ground is a surface electrical ground that is laid at a distance of 1 m and a depth of 0.5 m around the outer foundation of a building. In order to be effective, the ringer must be in contact with the earth along at least 80% of its total length.

Depending on the type of soil structure, however, all these earth grounders are subject to a greater or lesser degree of corrosion. Damage caused by earthworks can also not be ruled out.

In order to avoid these disadvantages, a foundation grounding system should be provided for new buildings. The foundation grounding is inserted into the building foundation and improves the efficacy for protection against electrical shock. The main potential equalization thus becomes far more effective.

The foundation earth electrode must be taken into account when contractors tender for structural work. Generally, the implementation is carried out by foundation manufacturers in conjunction with competent electricians. Since the foundation earth electrode is a component of the building's electrical system, responsible specialists of both trades should sign off on it before any concrete is employed on-site. Foundation earth electrode

A foundation earth electrode consists of non-insulated conductors, usually made of strip or round steel, embedded in the foundations of the exterior walls or in the floor slab of the building. It is connected to the earth across a large area via the relatively well-conducting concrete.

The foundation earth electrode must be executed as a closed ring ground. It must be connected to the main potential equalizing rail – usually in the house connection area – via a prominently marked, corrosion-resistant connecting jumper lug (hot-dip galvanized steel with plastic sheath or stainless steel) with a minimum length of 1.5 m. Additional connecting lugs must be provided to ensure lightning protection.

The galvanized or non-galvanized steel must be surrounded by at least 5 cm of concrete on all sides. This achieves a high level of corrosion resistance, which generally corresponds to the longevity of the building. Round bar steel should be at least 10 mm in diameter and strip steel (at least 30 × 3.5 mm or 25 × 4 mm) should be positioned upright.

In the case of large buildings, subdivision of the spanned surface area is recommended by creating cross-connections in widths of approximately 20 × 20 m. For terraced houses, a small closed ring should be formed beneath each house, depending on the size of the site.

In the case of waterproof concrete tanking, a "black tank" (sealed with bitumen), or a tank with perimeter insulation (thermal insulation), a ring ground outside the foundation is required to create a reliable connection with the earth. Please note that the ringer should be made of *stainless steel* as it is not surrounded by concrete and is therefore not protected against corrosion.

A prerequisite for effective overvoltage protection is electrical bonding. > Fig. 13 Electrical bonding is the practice of intentionally electrically connecting all exposed metallic items (housing) in a building that are not intended to carry electricity as protection from electric shock. Electrical bonding

Fig. 13: Electrical bonding rail with connecting lug (right)

Electrical bonding is usually installed in the basement, usually in the building's internal terminal box, and connects:

— the grounding/protective conductor of the electrical system,
— the grounding system,
— all dissipation of the excess voltage protection devices of the energy and computer networks,
— the conductive screens of wiring and cables,
— metal construction, gas, water, and heating systems, and
— the external lightning protection system.

ELECTRICAL CIRCUITS

The circuit is the total of all electrical loads supplied by the same distributor and protected by the same fuse. In residential buildings, each room is usually supplied with a circuit for luminaires and sockets. For household appliances such as electric cookers, ovens, dishwashers, washing machines, and so on, a separate circuit must be provided, even if the appliances are connected via sockets. Connections for three-phase, alternating current also receive their own circuits.

As with the number of sockets and connections, the number of circuits should correspond to the equipment values. If additional sockets and connections over and above the minimum are specified, then the number of circuits should be increased correspondingly.

Circuit distributors

Circuit distributors distribute the electrical energy already detected by the meter to the individual circuits. Installation distributors are used for this purpose. Installation distribution boards – also called residential distributors – are generally installed in apartments. In single-family houses, it is customary to combine circuit distributors and counters in one cabinet.

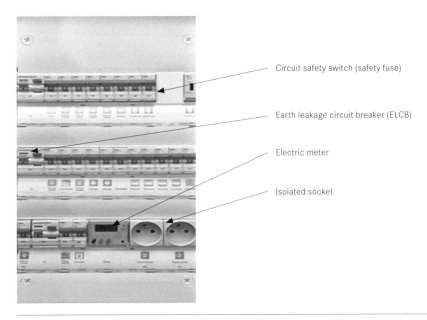

Circuit safety switch (safety fuse)

Earth leakage circuit breaker (ELCB)

Electric meter

Isolated socket

Fig. 14: Structure and arrangement of fittings in a distribution box

The following devices are accommodated in circuit distributors:

— Excess current protection devices, that is, line circuit breakers or fuses with a maximum rated current of 63 amperes
— Residual current circuit breaker
— Connection terminals
— Remote switch
— Switch contactors, time-delay switches, etc.

Most of these installations are designed in such a way that they can be clipped onto rails, so-called DIN rails, as a time-saving measure. Depending on the type of rooms in which the distributors are installed, safety categories from IP 30 (dry rooms) to IP 54 (for damp rooms or outdoors) are stipulated.

Distribution boards are available for wall mounting, recessed wall mounting, and cavity wall assembly (symbol: H). Since the dimensions of the products vary and do not correspond to the standard masonry dimensions, niches should be made large enough to accommodate a relatively large distribution box. Alternatively, it is necessary to coordinate at an early stage with the electrical installer regarding the product specification and its size. All cavities are plastered.

When planning distribution boards, it is important to make sure they are positioned in an easily accessible place. Because of the switching noise of relays and switchgear, distributor boxes should not be fitted in walls adjacent to bedrooms. The layout of the distribution boards should also correlate with the position and size of the house connection box or electrical room to permit optimal configuration of the wiring routes.

All control cabinets and distribution boards should be dimensioned with a 20% reserve tolerance for future components.

CONDUITS AND CABLES

Electrical energy is generally transported via wires and cables. It is transported from the power station via various intermediate stations to the electrical equipment and systems and then into the building.

Strands   A bundle of several strands in a sheath is referred to as a conduit. A wire is a conductor covered with plastic insulation. If a conductor is enclosed in an additional fixed coat, then it is referred to as a cable.

In residential buildings, copper cables are used exclusively. Alternating-current users are supplied with triple-wire, three-phase alternating current, or special circuits with 5-wire cables. The wires differ in their structure and their insulation, which is usually made from plastic or rubber. The wires are color-coded for ease of identification. The following combinations are generally used:

—   3 wires: green-yellow, black or brown, light blue
—   5 wires: green-yellow, black, light blue, brown, black

The green-yellow-colored conductor should be used strictly as a protective conductor (PE) or for the neutral conductor that has a protective function (PEN). > Chapter Earthing Systems

Cables and wires are marked with letter combinations, which provide information on the type and intended use. The plastic cable "NYY" is most frequently used in residential schemes. > Fig. 15

If a cable is to be used as a grounding cable, then it is covered with an additional plastic sheath. Such a grounding cable can then be placed directly in the ground.

Circuit networks and connections   The connection of wire cables with devices is primarily achieved by means of screw terminals and screwless terminals, though press connectors or plug connectors are also used. > Fig. 16

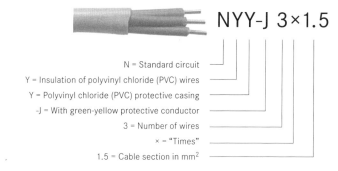

NYY-J 3×1.5

N = Standard circuit
Y = Insulation of polyvinyl chloride (PVC) wires
Y = Polyvinyl chloride (PVC) protective casing
-J = With green-yellow protective conductor
3 = Number of wires
× = "Times"
1.5 = Cable section in mm^2

Fig. 15: Annotated structure NYY-j 3 x1.5

Fig. 16: Connection options for electrical wiring

In principle, wire connections or junctions can only be carried out on an insulating mat or with an insulating covering. The connection points must remain accessible. Suitable terminal compartments – connecting sockets or boxes – are required for this. The route of the wiring varies, depending on the type of boxes used.

Cables are connected in special junction or device connection sockets.

WIRING LAYOUT

There are various options for the installation of electrical wiring:

Surface mount/flush installation

— visible as a surface-mounted installation,
— visible on installation channel systems, or
— concealed as a flush installation chased into the masonry or concrete,
— in wall cavities, or
— in installation ducts, underfloor ducts, or hollow floors.

Installation is forbidden in ventilation ducts or in chimney vents or flanks.

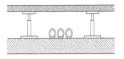
Raised floor

Underfloor conduit

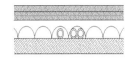
Cavity floor

Fig. 17: Concealed cable routing in floors

Wiring is predominantly flush-mounted in residential buildings. Here, cable routing is recommended in empty conduits, which allows for subsequent installations or extensions to be carried out without causing any damage.

In nonresidential buildings, the wiring is predominantly accommodated in suspended ceilings, raised floors, or parapet channels. > Fig. 17 This facilitates maintenance and allows for the flexible organization of switches, sockets, and lights, permitting, for example, a change in use.

INSTALLATION ZONES

In order to minimize conflicts with other connection pipes, such as gas, water, or heating conduits, and to prevent damage to cables, e.g., by drilling of dowel holes or nailing, cable routing of flush-mounted wires in walls is only installed vertically or horizontally. If possible, installations are also restricted to defined installation zones. Wiring in floors and ceilings, however, can be installed in the shortest possible way.

A low, horizontal installation zone is allocated in a 30-cm-wide zone, 30 cm above the floor, and a similar, upper horizontal installation zone runs below the ceiling. Light switches, sockets, and switches above working surfaces are arranged in a central horizontal installation zone. In the vicinity of door and window openings, and in the corner junctions of rooms, vertical installation zones have to be provided. Within these zones, in addition to the electrical wiring, it is preferable that connections, switches, and sockets be arranged centrally. > Fig. 18

When laying cables, special care must be taken to protect them from physical damage (which could lead to further injury and/or damage to property). This can be achieved either by their careful positioning or by the use of cover paneling.

Sockets, switches, or installation sockets located outside the installation zones must be supplied with a vertical branch cable extending from the nearest horizontal installation zone.

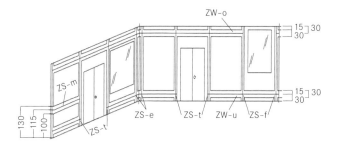

ZS-t: vertical installation zones around doorways:
10–30 cm from the building shell

ZS-f: vertical installation zones around windows:
10–30 cm from the building shell

ZS-e: vertical installation zones on the walls:
10–30 cm from the building shell

ZW-u: horizontal installation zones:
15–45 cm above the floor

ZW-o: horizontal installation zones:
15–45 cm below the ceiling finish

ZW-m: central horizontal installation zones:
100–130 cm above the floor

Fig. 18: Installation zones for electrical cables, switches, and sockets

INSTALLATION SYSTEMS

If cables are to be installed in a concealed manner, then no extensive fixing or protective equipment is required, as long as suitable cable types are installed. The cables can then be placed, for example, in walls and ceilings. Either slots are chiseled from walls and ceilings before plastering, so that cables can be installed flush to the surface, or flat cables are used, which can be fixed inside the plaster. > Fig. 19 Care ought to be taken not to compromise the loadbearing strength of the loadbearing elements when creating slots.

Flush-mounted installation

In drywall and gypsum-board walls, the wiring is usually installed in the cavity, so that initially only one side of the wall is built during the construction process and is then closed after the successful installation of all the wiring.

If there are no fire protection requirements on ceilings, then it is possible to route cables (e.g., for a light outlet) through holes in the floor above the ceiling. However, in this case, empty pipes should be used, to obviate the removal of the entire floor construction in the above story in case of subsequent installations.

Fig. 19: Installation methods for walls and ceilings

Fig. 20: Examples of grid channels (left), cable clips (right)

Fig. 21: Surface-mounted installation with an express clamp, cable clamp, cable collection holder, gripping iso-clamp, and empty conduit

The following cable structures and installation types are available for surface-mounted installations: > Figs. 20 and 21

— Cable channels
— Grid channels
— Conduit channels
— Cable conductors
— Collection brackets
— Cable clips
— Steel-armored conduits

For cost savings, cables are often routed in bundles in a single channel. > Fig. 22 This allows for access in the event of malfunctions and the ability to easily reinstall the cable. However, in order to ensure service reliability, the number of cables in a cable channel should be limited to the quantity authorized by the manufacturer. In particular, redundant systems should be routed in separate channels.

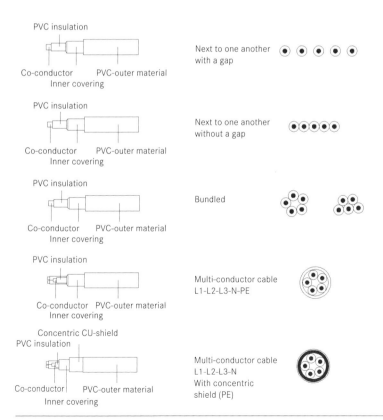

Fig. 22: Assembly and arrangement of wires in different cables

In certain instances, such as in office buildings, commercial complexes, or shopping centers, flexibility in the layout of units is an important parameter. This allows for changes in the energy distribution and the position of the power consumer. When they are laid visibly, cables allow this to a certain extent. However, this option is less visually pleasing and is comparatively complex. A less costly alternative is the use of rail distribution systems to distribute power.

The following table compares two energy distribution systems.

Tab. 4: Comparing rail and cable central power distribution

Characteristic	Rail distribution system (RDS)	Cable installation
Reaction to fire	Very low fire load density	Up to 10 times higher fire load of PVC cables than with SVS
Flexibility	Variable tap-off units; installation also possible under applied voltage	Changes and extension possible; installation work only possible in a "voltage-free" state
Material	Halogen-free rail boxes	Standard cables are not halogen or PVC free
Effort to install	Uncomplicated assembly with simple tools	Complex assembly with numerous auxiliary tools
Network installation	Linear design with outlets via tap-off units	A star-shaped supply of loads, thus cables accumulate at the feed-in point
Space requirements	Compact design, standardized angle, and offset elements	A lot of space is required for bending radius, type of layout, accumulation, and current load capacity
Price	Comparatively high installation costs	

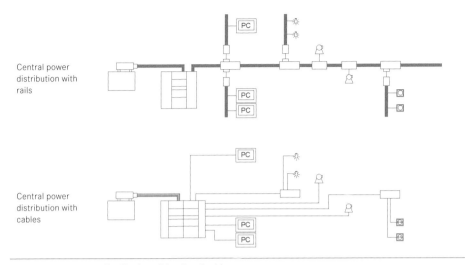

Central power
distribution with
rails

Central power
distribution with
cables

Fig. 23: Central power distribution with rail and cable

SOCKETS

Installation sockets are classified according to their intended use, as follows:

— Connection sockets – also known as distribution boxes or joint boxes – are used to accommodate connection terminals for conductors with a cross-section of up to 4 mm².
— Equipment sockets, so-called switch sockets, are used for mounting installation devices (switches, sockets, dimmers, actuators, etc.) in the wall and can also be used as connecting sockets without built-in devices.
— Device connection sockets – also known as appliance sockets or transit sockets – are intended for installation devices and additional connection terminals for through wiring.
— Sockets can be used with terminals for connecting a limited number of portable devices (such as electric heaters or wall lights) to the fixed installation.

Fig. 24: Conduit box

Fig. 25: Device connection boxes

Fig. 26: Shockproof plug

Conduit boxes

This standard form of installation provides for a separate junction box with a diameter of 70 mm and a depth corresponding to the device sockets for each connection point. This allows for subsequent changes or additions to the layout without great effort, thus requiring a relatively high investment in material, since more cables and branch outlets are required in order to use the conduit boxes.

Connection boxes

Connection boxes have sufficient space to accommodate the additional branching of cables in the device box for switches, sockets, dimmers, etc. This allows for a low-cost installation, since in this variation junction outlets are no longer required.

Shockproof sockets and plugs

Shockproof sockets and shockproof plugs are combined with three-wire connection cables to securely connect movable electrical devices with a protective conductor. Two opposite protective contacts in the socket and in the plug ensure a secure connection with the protective conductor. Thanks to their special geometrical design, it is guaranteed that during insertion the protective conductors of the plug and socket will always connect *before* the voltage-carrying sockets and plug pins.

In order to ensure that the protective measures in buildings are effective, shockproof sockets should be used. Socket inserts for flush mounting are available with hooks (e.g., for masonry or concrete) as well as with screw fastening (e.g., for drywalls). The attachment must be carried out in such a way that the socket cannot be pulled out of the mounting when the plug is removed. Also, the insulation of the conductors should not be damaged during installation.

Plugs, sockets, and extension cables (with plugs and coupling) must always be connected in such a way that the plug pins cannot be live under any circumstances when unplugged. Sockets, switches, remote control sockets, and so on are often combined with one another for functional reasons and due to their uniform design. In addition, they must be designed in such a way that the high-voltage part is protected against direct contact by separate, detachable covers. ■

SWITCHES

A wide variety of switches and sockets is available on the market. In residential installations these are often the only visible elements of the electrical installation. The variety, therefore, lies in particular with the design, as they can be adapted to any conceivable style of apartment or to the design and color of the walls. ■

Installation switches

Installation switches visible in the building, mounted in or on the wall, usually serve to switch light circuits on or off. A wide range of technical features is available with manually operated switches for fixed installations. Depending on the method of assessment, the following distinct types are available. According to the function, there are single, double, or triple-ended switches corresponding to basic circuits.

Circuits

■ **Tip**: In addition to the protective contact plugs, so-called "European plugs" fit into shockproof sockets. European plugs fit into sockets in all European countries.

■ **Tip**: Most manufacturers offer different sets of installation devices, each with a uniform design, often with a range of variations and combinations for different levels of interior design and requirements. It is therefore necessary to check if all necessary functions are covered by the desired switch series.

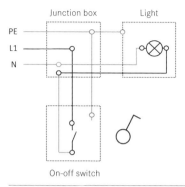

Fig. 27: Schematic diagram of the off-switch

— Off-switch, which is switched off from a switch point. This is the most common application in the private sector, where a luminaire is switched on or off with a switch. > Fig. 27

— Group switches, with which two luminaires are switched from one switching point, so that only one or the other luminaire is operated. Such a circuit is used, for example, for operating garage doors or blinds.

— Series switches, e.g., in versions with two compensators, where several lamps are switched on independently from a single switching point. Series switches are used, for example, in bathrooms to switch on mirror and ceiling lights. > Fig. 28

— Changeover switches – also called hall or hotel control – operate from two switching positions. This circuit is used in small lobbies or rooms with two entrances. > Fig. 29

— Intermediate switches can be operated from three or more switching positions. This connection consists of two changeover switches and any number of intermediate switches. These are mainly used in rooms with more than two entrances. > Fig. 30

The switches can usually be equipped with a glow control lamp (pilot light shines when the light is switched on) or with an orientation light (switch lighting, which shines when the light is switched off).

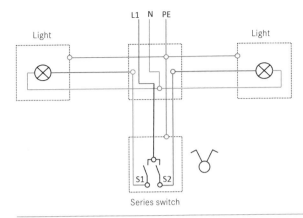

Fig. 28: Schematic diagram of the series circuit

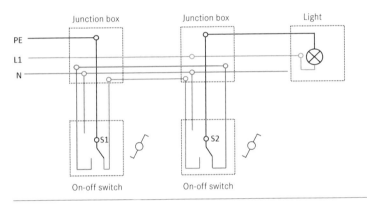

Fig. 29: Schematic diagram of changeover switches

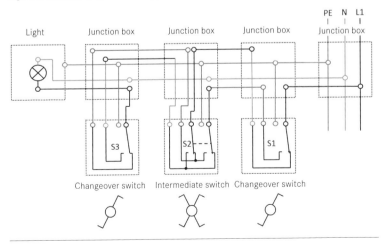

Fig. 30: Diagram of cross-connections

Fig. 31: Examples of rotational, rocking, tilting, push, and pull switches (from left to right)

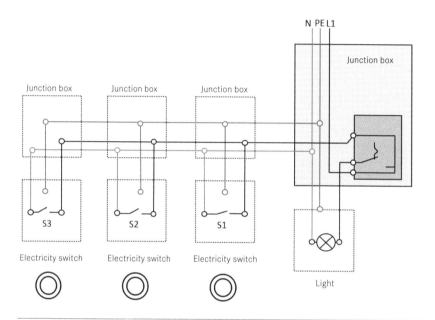

Fig. 32: Diagram of the impulse/push-button/relay circuit

According to the technical design, a distinction is made, for example, between rotational, rocker, tilting, push, and pull switches in the surface or flush-mounted design, also for cavity walls, door frames, and control panels. There are versions with screw covers and screwless covers, for rigid and flexible conductors. > Fig. 31

Special versions for different purposes include: push buttons for installation remote control, electronic switches, remote-controlled switches, switches in combination with dimmers, time switches, and so on.

Push-button   The so-called installation remote control is a light circuit with electromagnetic remote control, which functions with the aid of a latching relay. > Fig. 32 Instead of conventional switches (off, serial, change, and

Fig. 33: Variety of installation devices with uniform design (Source: Busch-Jaeger Elektro GmbH, Lüdenscheid)

cross-connections with corresponding wiring), simple push buttons are used here. A current surge circuit consists of the main circuit with the lights and the control circuit controlled by any number of push buttons.

When a push-button device is pressed, the installation remote switch, which is also referred to as an impulse switch or a current impulse relay, receives a pulse, or a current surge. This current surge triggers the switching operation in the circuit. The installation remote switch has two (or several) switching positions, which are changed by the pulses produced by the push buttons. At the next current surge, the following position is assumed. Installation remote switches are generally placed on the DIN rail in the circuit distributor.

The advantage of this is that any number of push buttons can be connected to the installation remote switch. This is particularly useful, for example, in long corridors or extended stairs, where you can control lights from various positions.

Dimmers are used to control the infinitely variable brightness of lighting. Dimmers differ in the manner in which they are operated (e.g., by rotating, by touch) and the type of light, since not every light can be combined with every kind of dimmer.

> Dimmers

In addition, there is a variety of special switches. These include, for example, key switches, motion detectors, twilight switches, and radio switches, which are generally also supplied by the manufacturer via the same switch programs. Furthermore, there are low-current elements for telephone, network, audio/video, intercom, loudspeakers, blinds, heating control, time switches, etc. > Fig. 33

> Other switch types

Protection against foreign bodies	1st digit	Moisture protection	2nd digit	Protection type	Example
d > 12.5 mm	2	None	0	IP 20	Socket in living area
d > 1.0 mm	4	Water splash	4	IP 44	Covered light in bath or shower
Dust	5	Water jet	5	IP 55	Distributor in a swimming pool

PROTECTION SYSTEMS

Sockets are required to house switches, sockets, dimmers, and so on, in walls. Equipment boxes for switches, sockets, or other devices are offered in flush-mounted versions and are not included in the purchased parts package for flush-mounted sockets or switches. On the other hand, surface-mounted appliance sockets are usually included as part of the installation equipment, e.g., for the installation of damp-proof installations that have protection grade IP 44.

LIGHTING SYSTEMS

In addition to fixtures for general and accent lighting, lighting systems also include fixtures for safety lighting (safety lighting system, safety light, single-battery light).

In addition to safety lighting, which usually has its own, secured circuit, all cables for luminaires must be integrated into the layout planning. Here, it is specifically the routing of the light outlets that should be planned when, for example, ceiling lights need to be arranged in exposed concrete ceilings. Some luminaire types function with low-voltage systems or ballasts, so that the setting of the luminaires and lights is useful at an early stage in the planning process. Recessed luminaires are often installed in hollow boxes, which need to be fitted at the same time as the concreting of the ceiling. > Fig. 35 Rapid developments in the area of LEDs mean that lighting concepts can be completely reconceived due to the longevity and extremely low current requirement of LEDs.

○ **Note**: Lighting systems and coordination with natural daylighting are described in detail in *Basics Lighting Design*, part of this series. Therefore, only the relevant content for electrical planning is discussed here.

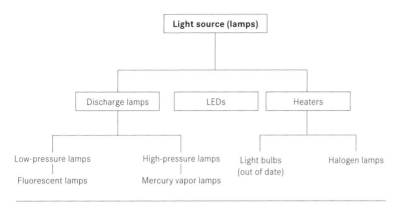

Fig. 34: Classification of light sources

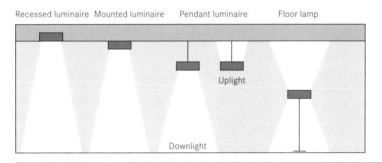

Fig. 35: Types of luminaires

Emergency lighting is required in the event that the power supply to the general artificial lighting fails. Therefore, power sources for emergency lighting must be planned independently from the power supply for general artificial lighting. When designing the emergency lighting, a distinction is made between safety lighting and replacement lighting. In order to meet safety regulations, safety lighting must fill the following roles in the event of a failure of the general power supply, to ensure that people can safely leave a building, to avoid panic, and to ensure safety in potentially perilous workplaces: > Tab. 6

Emergency lighting

Tab. 6: Structural systems for emergency lighting

Facilities where people congregate	Switch-over time max. (S)	Rated operating time Power source for safety purposes (h)	Lit or backlit Safety symbols in continuously operated buildings	Central Power Supply System (CPS)	Power supply system with service description	Single battery system	Power generation unit without interruption (0 s)	Power generation unit short interruption (<0.5 s)	Power generation unit medium interruption (<15 s)
Public places, theaters, restaurants, airports, railroad stations	1	3	X	X	X	X	X	X	
Hotels, hostels	15	8	X	X	X	X	X	X	X
Schools, high-rise buildings, underground garages, parking lots	15	3	X	X	X	X	X	X	X
Rescue routes in workplaces	15		X	X	X	X	X	X	X
High-risk workplaces	0.5		X	X	X	X	X	X	

— Lighting or backlighting of safety signs for escape routes
— Illumination of rescue routes
— Lighting of firefighting and signaling systems
— Facilitation of rescue operations

Depending on the specifications, a separate, fire-retardant cable network may be required. This can be arranged in F90 components without a fire load or as a protected E30/E90 cable. If necessary, battery solutions can also be used.

Safety lighting ought to be provided, among other reasons, to illuminate rescue routes in workplaces, accommodation facilities, homes, restaurants, and public places such as theaters, stages, cinemas, exhibition halls, underground garages and parking lots, airports and train stations, as well as schools.

Standby lighting Replacement lighting is used so that economically and/or technically important work can be carried out in the event of the failure of normal lighting. Therefore, the requirements applicable to safety lighting must be met and, furthermore, the power of the replacement lighting must correspond to the power of the normal lighting. At lower lighting levels, standby lighting can only be used to shut down or halt work processes.

Lightning Protection Systems

Surge voltages are short-term voltage impulses – so-called "tran- Excess voltage
sients" (from Latin *transire*, "past") – that occur for only fractions of a
second. These achieve voltage values of several 10,000 volts. They have
very short rise times of a few microseconds (µs) before they drop relatively slowly over a period of up to several 100 µs.

The causes of voltage surges are:

— direct or indirect lightning pulses at distances of up to several
   kilometers (LEMP, lightning electromagnetic pulse)
— switching operations in the energy network or in residences
   (SEMP, switching electromagnetic pulse)
— electrostatic discharge (ESD, electrostatic discharge)

In the case of a lightning strike, it is usually assumed that approximately 50% of the lightning current is discharged into the earth via the
external lightning protection system (lightning arrester). Up to 50% of the
remaining lightning current flows into the building via electrically conductive systems such as the main potential equalization. Therefore, despite the presence of an external lightning protection system, it is always
necessary to install an internal lightning protection system as well.

External lightning protection is formed by means of structural meas- External lightning protection
ures such as capturing devices, static eliminators (lightning arresters), and
earthing systems. > Figs. 36 and 37 It protects buildings only against mechan-
ical damage and fire; it does not prevent the rise of the electrical potential
of the building hit by the lightning to around tenfold, from approximately
a few 10 kV to some 100 kV compared with the environment. These potential differences exceed the insulation resistance of low-voltage consumer
systems many times over, frequently resulting in their total destruction.

Internal lightning protection, on the other hand, is implemented by Internal lightning protection
means of protective elements such as a lightning arrester (so-called
coarse protection), a surge diverter (medium protection), and device protection (fine protection).

A risk analysis is required for risk management based on lightning
protection. This initially determines the need for lightning protection.
Later, technically and economically optimal protection measures will be
defined. The building in question is subdivided into one or more lightning
protection zones (LPZ).

Fig. 36: Lightning conductor on a house

Fig. 37: Lightning protection devices mounted on the roof

Lightning protection zones

The protection zones are defined as follows:

Zone 0 (LPZ 0): In this area, outside a building, there is no protection against electromagnetic interference impulses (LEMP). There is a differentiation between the two LPZ 0 areas: LPZ 0A refers to the area subject to impact. Here, there are aboveground devices and wiring outside buildings and areas of protection. LPZ 0B, on the other hand, refers to the area protected from direct lightning strike by an external lightning protection system. Affected are: underground cables, external devices, and cables within 20 m of the protection zone of the building, or devices and cables more than 20 m outside the protection zone, if they are situated within the protection area of a lightning protection system or an insulated air-termination system.

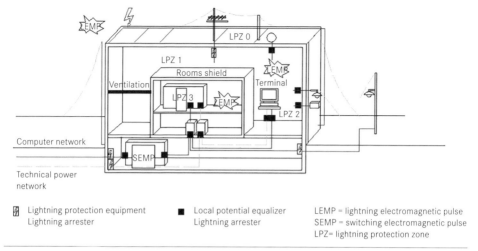

Computer network

Technical power
network

	Lightning protection equipment	■	Local potential equalizer	LEMP = lightning electromagnetic pulse
	Lightning arrester		Lightning arrester	SEMP = switching electromagnetic pulse
				LPZ= lightning protection zone

Fig. 38: Protection zone concept in lightning protection

Zone 1 (LPZ 1): The transition from LPZ 0B to LPZ 1 is effected by means of a lightning current arrester that can be installed, for example, in the main distributor or at the entrance to the building and which pro-vides protection from direct or nearby lightning strikes. Zone 1 relates to equipment and cables within buildings (including basements).

Zone 2 (LPZ 2): The transition from LPZ 1 to LPZ 2 is effected by means of a lightning arrester that is installed, for example, in the current distribution or sub-distribution and protects it against excess voltages caused by lightning strikes over the supply network. Zone 2 only miti-gates for slight voltage excesses.

Zone 3 (LPZ 3): The transition from LPZ 2 to LPZ 3 is effected by means of a device protection, that is, a mobile surge arrester, which can be installed, for example, on sockets or electrical devices. It protects against excess voltages in the power supply of the end user. In Zone 3 there are no interfering impulses due to LEMP or excess voltage.

For each lightning zone, the geometric limits, the lightning data, and the type of damage to be considered are specified. The assumed risk is reduced by the use of protective measures until an acceptable residual risk is reached, proceeding from the unprotected state of the object. Pro-tective measures must be considered for, on the one hand, structural in-stallations, the people within the building, and electrical and electronic equipment and, on the other hand, for the supply circuits.

Low-Voltage Installations in Buildings

Low-voltage systems are electrical installations which, as a rule, do not carry currents that are hazardous for humans or can cause serious damage to property. In practice, such low-current systems function with voltages of less than 50 volts and currents of less than 2 amps.

NETWORK AND COMMUNICATIONS TECHNOLOGY

Phone/Internet connection

The connection of a building to the external communications technology usually takes place via a telephone/ISDN or DSL connection, if necessary also over high-capacity glass-fiber or satellite connections. The telephone network provider installs a line in the house. Additional networking of the connection sockets in residences or other buildings takes place within the framework of electrical planning. Usually, a telephone connection unit (TAE socket) is installed in the apartment or unit at a central location, from where routers manage the internal network operation with Internet, telephone, fax, etc.

Router solutions in residential buildings

In apartments, routers are normally connected to the TAE socket, which has additional connections for analog terminals (telephone, fax, etc.) and network cables. Other devices can be integrated into the communications network by radio-based means via Wireless Local Area Network (WLAN) and Digital Enhanced Cordless Telecommunications (DECT). In upmarket housing, it is now customary to supply all rooms with Ethernet cabling and to provide corresponding sockets as well as a patch field in the area of the telephone/Internet connection for setting up a home network.

Server solutions

In larger buildings, such as office buildings, more complex network systems are built, which generally have their own server cabinets/racks or server rooms. All LAN-bound data cables are distributed from this point into the units, resulting in a high installation density in the area of the servers and patch fields. > Figs. 39 and 40 If necessary, separate rooms are planned for central usage units (such as enterprise-wide data storage), which can have autonomous energy and air supply, fire protection measures, and high security standards for accessibility.

Server cabinets/racks

The central units of a network are the server cabinets (also called racks), which usually have an installation dimension of 19 inches (approx. 48 cm) and 21 inches (approx. 53 cm). The outer dimensions of server cabinets are usually 60 cm or 80 cm wide and stand-alone cabinets are usually between 200 cm and 220 cm high. The depth varies between 60 cm and 120 cm, depending on the installation components and on

Fig. 39: Network sockets RJ45

Fig. 40: Networking a Local Area Network (LAN)

Fig. 41: Network cable CAT with an RJ45 plug (left) and a fiber-optic cable (right)

whether they have two-sided operability. A 100 cm-wide area in front of and behind the server cabinets should be provided for their installation and maintenance. In smaller units, only patch fields can be used, which can easily be accommodated inside cabinets.

A typical Ethernet cabling consists of RJ45 patch cables or optical fibers (FO) > Fig. 41, which connect the network distributor/patch panel to the socket or terminal. It is usually practical to configure the cabling of networks in such a way that access to the cables is provided during operation for maintenance and exchange purposes. This can be done by means of cavity conduction paths (in cable ducts, cable planks, or double-layer/hollow floors) or empty conduits.   Ethernet

An alternative that is increasingly specified is networking via the sockets of the existing low-voltage installation (also called power LAN). Here, additional cabling of networks can be dispensed with.   Power LAN

Door and room-to-room communication generally comprises speech and video systems for entrance doors. In addition to the simple buzzer, which allows door opening via an electrical voltage, there are various communication systems. Intercom devices are usually situated radially outward from the doorbell of the entrance door to listener intercom systems at the entrance doors of the apartments or units. However, they do not allow communication between one another. Hands-free devices, on the other hand, do not require a handset and can also be mounted as a home communication system. Additional video features are often added nowadays, which make it possible to view the caller without the necessity for audio contact. However, extra video cabling is necessary for this.

TV reception can be via Internet, cable, satellite, or antenna. Cable connections are placed parallel to the telecommunication via the street into the house, while antenna reception is usually decentralized. The use of satellite systems requires more precise planning of the route and the positioning of the parabolic antenna, since this must have an undisturbed, direct connection to the satellite for interference-free reception.

The classic distribution of video / audio signals in houses is via coaxial cables and corresponding sockets. > Fig. 42 Coaxial cables (abbreviated: coax cables) are bipolar cables with a concentric composition. They consist of an inner conductor (also called a soul) that is surrounded at a constant distance by a hollow, cylindrical outer conductor. The outer conductor shields the inner conductor from interference radiation. Today, digital lines are standard on most end devices, enabling network connections to be used. In addition, loudspeaker cabling is installed in a flush manner to ensure high-quality transmission paths from amplifiers to loudspeakers.

○ **Note**: The current, standard digital video broadcasting (DVB) is differentiated according to the following categories:
- DVB-C: connection via cable
- DVB-S: connection via satellite reception
- DVB-T: terrestrial connection via antenna

Fig. 42: Connection sockets for coaxial and loudspeaker cables

ELECTROACOUSTIC SYSTEMS

Apart from voice alarm systems (VAS), electroacoustic systems (EAS) also include electroacoustic emergency warning systems and public address systems (PA). If possible, the entire electroacoustic system should be available in a building to perform different functions. For instance:

— Emergency call and announcements with freely selectable and programmable gong introductions
— Targeted alarming with evacuation instructions
— Music transmission with high sound quality

For this purpose, the device is divided into loudspeaker circuits for individual calls to all the auxiliary rooms. When connected to a loudspeaker circuit, the switched programs in the remaining areas should not be interrupted.

The triggering of an alarm signal by the fire alarm system should take place automatically in the event of an emergency, using preprogrammed loudspeaker lines. A common hazard signal is used as an alarm signal. Targeted evacuation instructions are stored digitally as a sound file and are automatically triggered in the respective building sections by the fire detection function of the fire alarm center via monitored interfaces.

Sub-master stations in remote buildings with independent programs must be connected to the main center and integrated into the monitoring of the main center. External systems for music recording as well as background music programs via the alarm system are to be muted to ensure high speech intelligibility in the event of an emergency.

For the mobilization and evacuation of personnel, police and fire-fighters need an emergency system that remains functioning in an emergency. The alarm system is therefore to be equipped with a UPS system, which ensures functionality for at least thirty minutes. The reserve power supply must also be considered.

VIDEO SURVEILLANCE

Video surveillance is the observation of objects, people, or property by video camera and monitor. Video surveillance is usually designed in a closed system via fixed cables (closed-circuit television, or CCTV).

In the simplest form of video surveillance, only a video camera and monitor are connected. Depending on the required task, however, it might be necessary to integrate additional components into the video surveillance system.

Analog video

In the case of analog video systems, the video system signals (video, control, and parameterization) are transmitted via coax cables or two-wire lines, or modulated via glass fiber. The information of these signals consists of analog (non-graduated) voltage values in the transmitted frequency. In traditional analog video systems, numerous cameras with crossbars are connected to numerous monitors. This results in a point-to-point connection, the signal direction of which has already been defined in the planning phase.

The cabling is usually star-shaped, allowing subunits (satellite systems) to be formed. The quality of the analog video is generally high. If, however, the analog video signal is transmitted over longer distances, the signal level decreases and the image loses contrast. Likewise, high-frequency components are dulled, which results in increasing loss of clarity. If additional amplifiers (equalizers) are used, then the signal noise increases. Video quality therefore decreases with increasing transmission distance.

Video over IP (VioIP)

In contrast to analog video, video system signals are digital at video IP and are transmitted via an IT network (local/wide area network – LAN/WAN – or Internet). These IT networks typically consist of active components (switchboards, routers, etc.) and interconnections. These are usually UTP (Unshielded Twisted Pair) cables, balanced, unshielded cables with twisted and colored paired wires (Cat 5, 6, or 7), fiber (optical fiber), or wireless connections.

The quality of the IT network digital video signal is independent of the distance of the transmission path and is thus always maintained. The direction of the signal path is determined by the terminal used (camera, monitor, recorder, etc.) and can therefore be changed. Thus, it is also possible to integrate other devices into the IT network, provided that the permissible network load in the affected sector is not exceeded.

HAZARD WARNING AND ALARM SYSTEMS

Hazard warning systems are used to reliably recognize and report danger to people and property. > Fig. 43 They automatically or manually trigger the processing, transmission, and emission of danger reports. The transmission paths in ring technology or DC technology are permanently monitored.

Burglar alarm systems are hazard detection systems that automatically monitor property for theft, as well as for unauthorized entry into areas and rooms. If the building envelope is to be monitored, then magnetic contacts, sensors, motion detectors, and glass break detectors, etc., must be integrated into the system. In their planning, architects must take into consideration that all windows, doors, and other entrance openings must be suitably electrified.

Burglar alarm systems

Burglary and holdup alarm systems are hazard detection systems that are used to make a direct call for help in case of an attack – usually directly to the police. Furthermore, this alarm can also be used as a secondary alarm by an external safety control unit.

Burglary and holdup alarm systems

Fire detection systems are hazard detection systems that are used to make a direct call in the event of a fire or to report a fire at an early stage.

Fire detection systems

These systems consist of fire detectors, a fire alarm control center with access to an emergency power supply, a transmission device, alarm devices for internal alarm, and control devices, which close fire protection doors, open smoke and heat outlets, control fire extinguishing systems, switch off machines, and so on.

The role of automatic fire detectors is to detect evidence of fire, such as visible or invisible smoke, heat, or flames, and to report this to the fire detection center.

One distinguishes between the sizes of fires depending on optical, thermal, and chemical fire detectors or combinations thereof, flame detectors, and special detectors and smoke suction systems. In addition, there are also handheld detectors that are used on escape routes for the manual triggering of alarms. The detectors are connected individually or in groups for the transmission of signals. These are routed to the fire alarm center as a branch and/or ring line.

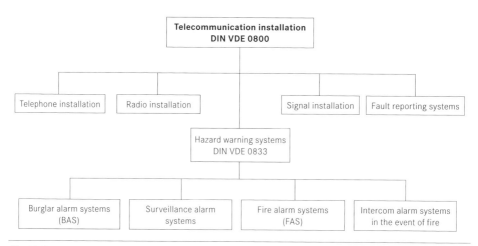

Fig. 43: Structural classification of hazard reporting systems

The fire detection center records, evaluates, and processes the pre-tested signals from the detectors. In the event of a fire, the optical and acoustic signaling of the triggering detectors via the transmission device is sent to the fire department or somewhere that can provide assistance. Precise fire detection is achieved through the use of targeted detectors. Further tasks of the fire detection center include functional monitoring of the entire system and warning of possible faults, as well as activation of electrically controlled extinguishing systems.

In addition to extensive fire alarm systems in larger buildings, smoke detectors should be installed in apartments. These should be attached to ceilings in all living rooms and bedrooms. Here, cable-free battery solutions are also an option. > Fig. 44 High-quality smoke detectors can also be connected so that, in the event of an incident, all smoke detectors can give a signal simultaneously.

Voice alarm systems   To alert individuals or the occupants of an entire building, the use of acoustic signal generators with DIN-tone is preferable. > Fig. 45 In production areas with sound levels exceeding 110 dB(A) and in public areas, optical signal transmitters are also required, since hearing-impaired people must also be taken into consideration. Optical alarm devices include revolving signal lights or flashing lights.

Acoustic alarm devices for fire warnings include: sirens, horns, electronic signal transmitters with adjustable tones, PA systems, and voice alarm systems.

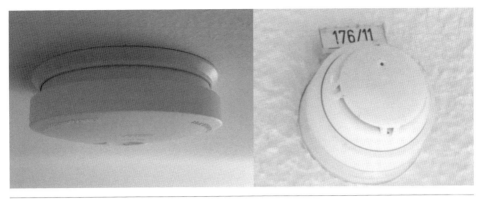

Fig. 44: Smoke detector (left) and fire detector (right)

Fig. 45: Alarm installation loudspeaker in a suspended ceiling

Building Automation

BUS SYSTEMS

Facilities that are used for the automatic control and monitoring of technical installations and processes in buildings, as well as for checking their consumption data, are grouped under the term "building automation." The system is divided into three areas: > Fig. 47 and Chapter Levels of Building Automation

1. Management level
2. Automation level
3. Field level

Building system engineering/bus technology should be regarded as part of building automation, which carries out automatic functions within the premises of the building. This is possible across rooms, within a building, and between separate buildings. The concept of building automation emerged in order to differentiate it from conventional electrical installations. The previous installation of individual components has now been replaced by systems technology, or the "system bus."

In contrast to conventional electrical installations, the two-core, low-current bus system is used for information transmission and, irrespective of its low-voltage supply, carries the circuit of the terminals. Sensors send the recorded information to the actuators, which convert it into switching signals for the terminals (e.g., air conditioning). > Fig. 46 Since all actuators and sensors are connected to the same line, complex control processes can be managed via a single (bus) system. The most important bus systems are EIB/KNX, LON, and LCN.

EIB/KNX   EIB/KNX was originally developed under the auspices of the European Installation Bus (EIB) as a common standard for the application of building automation in commercial and residential buildings. After the system was modified, it came onto the market as KNX. KNX is the only global standard that enables the connection of products from different manufacturers. The system consists of so-called "participants": the sensors and the actuators. Sensors detect physical variables such as temperature, pressure, or air pressure, convert them into information, and pass it on to the network. Actuators receive this information, convert it into physical quantities, and trigger a function, for example with lamps, heaters, or blinds.

The smallest unit of a KNX system is a line. This can consist of a maximum of 64 participants and can have a maximum length of 100 m.

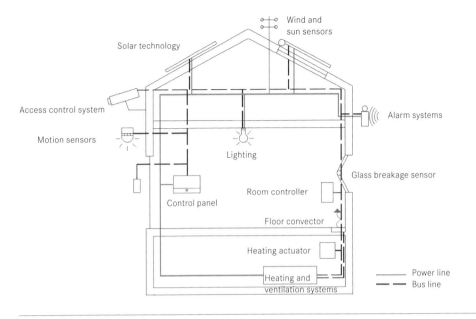

Fig. 46: Application areas of building automation

LON

The origin of the Local Operating Network (LON) was decentralized automation with the help of a control unit, which can be used for all devices, so-called "nodes." In addition to sensors and actuators, there are also controllers in a LON. In this way, information that is only required locally is also processed locally. LONs are mainly used in measurement and control engineering (MSR). This technique is rarely found for domestic technology such as heating, ventilation, and air conditioning.

LCN

The Local Control Network (LCN) is also used in building automation. In this system, the sensors and actuators are equipped with microcomputers that are compact enough to fit into sub-distribution boxes or circuit distribution. The LCN is characterized by the ease with which it can be planned, installed, and programmed – not least as the sensors and actuators can be accommodated in a module.

The 230 V network is used as a bus, but it ought to be equipped with an additional wire. If this is taken into account during the electrical installation, then no further cabling is required. Also, the LCN modules do not require power supplies as they are connected directly to the power cables. An LCN segment consists of a maximum of 250 modules, which allows several hundred rooms to be controlled on a regular basis.

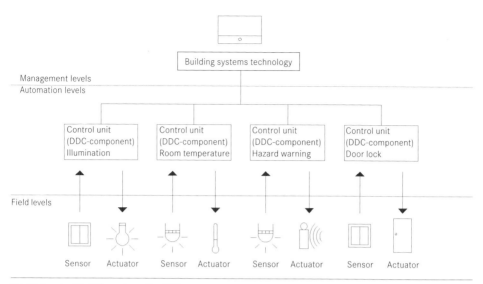

Fig. 47: Levels of building automation (BA)

LEVELS OF BUILDING AUTOMATION

The three levels of a BA system mentioned above are distinguished by the size and complexity of the building or the properties to be automated. Due to advances in digital control and control technology, the boundaries between the levels are becoming increasingly blurred. Functions of the automation level have become increasingly decentralized with more powerful digital systems, that is to say, integrated into the various zone levels.

Field level   At the lowest field level of the building, its various technical installations are operated with the help of the field devices: sensors and actuators. Sensors record information and transmit it to the actuators via a bus system (see above). The actuators receive the data and convert it into switching signals. Information is processed at the field level and prepared for the higher levels.

Automation level   With its control units (DDC – Direct Digital Control), the automation level monitors the limit values, switching states, counter reading, control, and regulation of the building's technical installations. Automation stations process the resulting data and communicate it to the field or management levels. These are small, powerful devices that can be implemented in digital technology and configured with standardized software tools.

The management level involves the higher-level operation and monitoring of activities and the signaling of faults should they occur. Information on building automation is collected here and evaluated, for example,
on the terminal screen and printed out on the log printer. The management level includes the implementation of system-wide and high-level control and optimization algorithms. In addition to a computer, the necessary
equipment includes a redundant data storage incorporating possibilities
for data backup and, if necessary, an uninterrupted power supply.

HIGH-LEVEL MANAGEMENT FUNCTIONS

A management system can be implemented as a central control room
or as distributed systems with several operator stations based on client-
server architecture. The management system software consists of a multi-
tasking operating system, a powerful database system, user software,
and process visualization software. The software communicates between
the management and automation levels via a defined transfer point – the
building automation node – and exchanges data with its databases.

The use of high-level management functions requires the intercon-
nection of all related BA systems into an interoperable system, which
must be available for the connection of various systems. For this purpose, the system requires an open communications interface such as,
for example, the neutral data transmission system FND or the BACnet,
so that, if required, it is possible to connect further automation devices
to the operating and management devices.

BACnet/IP provides a method for BACnet automation networks to
expand over building and property boundaries. An Ethernet network,
which is generally used for data transport, is set up via routers, hubs,
switches, repeaters, and transceivers.

A BACnet/IP network is a virtual network consisting of one or more
IP subnetworks (IP domains) that share the same BACnet network number. It contains a number of nodes that communicate using the BACnet/
IP protocol. The BACnet/IP nodes may belong to different physical networks, which in turn are part of a larger IP network and are exclusively
connected by IP routers. Several BACnet/IP nodes can belong to the
same BACnet network.

With the help of bus systems, control systems for lighting, roller shutters and blinds, heating, etc., can be installed and programmed easily,
using fewer cables. All devices and systems in the building communicate
via the bus line. Central functions use this line and control a selected
number of devices, or all of them, via a single control command – the bus
telegram. The corresponding bus commands have to be programmed.

Examples of central functions:

- All lights in the building on or off
- Close all windows
- Lower the thermostatic valves of the heaters
- Close or open blinds

All functions can be combined as desired. In conventional installations, for example, a central switching off of the lighting in conjunction with the down-regulation of the heaters would only be possible with additional wiring. If a bus system is to be installed, then the contractor must inform the system integrator who is programming and commissioning the system of the specific connections required. Some examples:

- "Lights off": all the lights in the house are simultaneously switched off by pushing the button when sleeping. Individual lighting, such as aquarium lighting, can be excluded.
- "Lights on": all lights are switched on, either by pressing the button or automatically, e.g., when the alarm system is activated.
- "Heating on/off": when leaving or entering the house, all radiators are adjusted down or up to a predefined value (e.g., anti-freeze position).
- "Blinds up/down": in the morning and in the evening or automatically, such as during storms (signal from the wind monitor), all blinds are raised and all awnings retracted.
- "Close windows": when a person leaves the house, all windows do not have to be checked individually; they all close at once or automatically with corresponding signals from the rain/wind monitor.
- "Leaving the house": for safety reasons, all electrical appliances (except refrigerators and freezers) are switched off; lights are switched off (except aquarium lighting); all windows are closed; blinds are switched to the random mode to make it look as if the house is occupied; radiators are reduced to a minimum.

The ability to program central functions can contribute to energy savings. They can also be operated remotely – via Internet, mobile phone, and so on – for example to switch on the heating before arrival.

Comfort functions   In addition to increased safety and energy savings, one of the primary objectives of building automation is to achieve a higher level of comfort for the user. A high degree of automation is achieved when the BA system automatically adjusts to the user's predefined settings and, under normal circumstances, does not require manual user interventions. Some examples:

- Brightness- and presence-controlled switching, which switches lighting on or off with the aim of creating uniformly lit spaces when people are present in the room.
- Storage of "scenes" that can be activated at the push of a button depending on the use of the space, for example dimming down the light and/or closing the shutters when a presentation is given in a seminar room.
- Use- and presence-activated heating control, where the desired comfort temperature is automatically controlled and maintained.
- Automatic control of the blinds according to sunlight, so that glare does not occur and/or the rooms are not overheated during the summer period.

Implementation of Electrical Planning

Electrical planning includes the sum of all electrical wiring, connections, and other elements. Even though most elements of electrical planning might play a key role in the planning and the determination of qualities, the requirements of electrical planning must be integrated into the design right from the outset.

The location and dimensioning of the house connection area and the cable routes are particularly important parameters in the design process. In addition, early predefinition – for example, regarding the extent of electrification of components – enables architects to estimate heights of ceiling and floor constructions, in order to determine room proportions and overall building heights.

Thus, close coordination between electrical planning, architectural design, and the other technical planning with experts during the planning process is necessary in order to attain a holistic solution.

PLAN OF EXECUTION

Ultimately, the project planning should result in the implementation of all of the contractor's functional specifications. Moreover, the plan of execution should be so clear and comprehensive that the contractor can derive the assembly planning from it without having to carry out any further calculations or measurements. In addition to the electro-planning based on the architecture planning and electrical drawings, the calculation and determination of systems, and definition of quality levels are also necessary. > Figs. 48 and 49

Special attention must be paid to coordination with other trades. This doesn't only mean that the planning is carried out to a high technical level and on schedule; but the various trades companies must not obstruct one another. Care must be taken to prevent clashes, particularly with other domestic engineering trades. This applies in particular to the management of cabling routes, but also to fire partitioning and the positioning of slots, recesses, and ducts.

DIMENSIONING

With regard to the electrical power supply, estimation of the required power is the most important task in the basic determination. In order to achieve high efficiency, the components should operate at a capacity of approximately 70% to 80% of maximum power. Insufficient dimensioning leads to malfunctions and excess dimensioning to inflated costs.

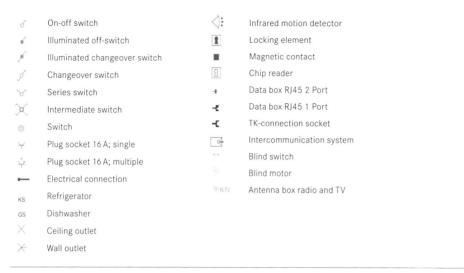

♂	On-off switch	◁:	Infrared motion detector
♂	Illuminated off-switch	🔒	Locking element
♂	Illuminated changeover switch	■	Magnetic contact
♂	Changeover switch	🔲	Chip reader
✓	Series switch	⊣	Data box RJ45 2 Port
✗	Intermediate switch	⊏	Data box RJ45 1 Port
◎	Switch	⊏	TK-connection socket
⊻	Plug socket 16 A; single	🔲	Intercommunication system
⊻	Plug socket 16 A; multiple		Blind switch
▬	Electrical connection		Blind motor
KS	Refrigerator	R.TV	Antenna box radio and TV
GS	Dishwasher		
✕	Ceiling outlet		
✻	Wall outlet		

Fig. 48: Annotation symbols in electrical planning

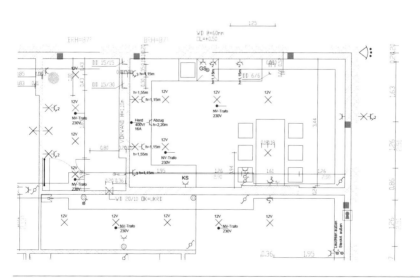

Fig. 49: Detail of an electrical plan

67

The dimensioning of networks and electrical systems is undertaken via the so-called "power requirement calculation," which takes into account the connections that the respective installation components have. In order to be able to configure the installation components, user requirements, building regulations, technical equipment, and technical installations for the design planning must first be compiled roughly and then compiled in detail for the execution planning.

The total connection value of the building is calculated as the sum of the connected values of individual devices. This represents the maximum required electrical power. Examples of the electrical values of electrical appliances in a typical residential building are shown in Tab. 8.

The power requirement is determined as the sum of the installed capacity (ascertained by the electrical supply data) and the concurrency factor. The fact that not all electrical equipment or electrical systems are simultaneously switched on or operated at full load is taken into account. The concurrency factor "g" is the ratio of the power consumed at a point of the network, or the electrical system, to the power installed behind this location.

Tab. 8 contains benchmark values of the concurrency factor for residential buildings and public buildings. These assessment values are not concrete, project-specific values, since individual energy requirements lead to entirely different factors, taking daily and annual changes into account in specific cases. For dimensioning, the least favorable load case – that is, the case with the highest simultaneous energy requirement – should be determined.

In addition to electrical household appliances, sockets, outlets, and connections should also be taken into account during planning. Every living room, dining room, and bedroom should be equipped equally, with at least one socket per wall. Each room should be equipped with at least one switch for the lighting. Sockets near water, e.g., in kitchens, bathrooms, and garages, must be fitted with a residual current device (RCD).

Depending on the equipment, electrical installations in residential buildings should be provided with a minimum of sockets, outlets, and connections. > Tab. 9

The value of the equipment is generally defined for a single residential unit. Each individual room must correspond to the respective minimum requirements of the equipment value according to its use. The allocation of space is possible once the value has been defined.

Tab. 7: Power consumption of household appliances

Household appliance		Connection value in [W]	
		from	to
iron	Alternating current	12,000	1,000
water heater	3-phase current	2,500	21,000
built-in oven	3-phase current	6,000	5,000
built-in cooker	3-phase current	8,000	8,500
electric oven	3-phase current	1,600	14,000
fryer	Alternating current	120	2,300
freezer	Alternating current	3,000	200
dishwasher	Alternating current	700	4,500
coffee machine	Alternating current	100	1,200
fridge	Alternating current	1,000	130
microwave oven	Alternating current	4,500	2,000
sauna	3-phase current	300	18,000
vacuum cleaner	Alternating current	1,000	1,000
hot water storage 15 l – 30 l	3-phase current	1,000	4,000
hot water storage 50 l – 150 l	3-phase current	3,000	6,000
clothes dryer	Alternating current	2,000	3,600
washing machine	Alternating current	2000	3,300

Tab. 8: Simultaneity factors for the main feed

Type of building	Concurrency factor	
	from	to
Residential building		
Single-family houses	0.4	0.4
Multifamily houses		
— General requirements (without electric heating)	0.6	0.6
— Electrical heating and air conditioning	0.8	1.0
Public building		
Hotels, guesthouses, etc.	0.6	0.8
Small offices	0.5	0.7
Large offices	0.7	0.8
Shops	0.5	0.7
Schools, etc.	0.6	0.7
Hospitals	0.5	0.75
Meeting rooms	0.6	0.8

Tab. 9: Equipment values for electrical installations in residential buildings
(according to RAL-RG 678)

Equipment value	Identification	Quality
1	*	Minimum equipment according to DIN 18015-2
2	**	Standard equipment
3	***	Convenience equipment
1 plus	* plus	Minimum equipment according to DIN 18015-2 and preparation for the use of building system technology according to DIN 18015-4
2 plus	** plus	Standard equipment and at least one functional area according to DIN 18015-4
3 plus	*** plus	Convenience equipment and at least two functional areas according to DIN 18015-4

The equipment value is ascertained according to the number of sockets, the lighting connections, and the telephone and radio/TV/data connections for the different room types in the living area. Indicated in Fig. 50 and 51 below are the equipment values proportional to the number of sockets > Fig. 50 and lighting connections > Fig. 51.

CALCULATIONS

Calculations made in the design planning are constantly updated on the basis of findings obtained during the course of detailed planning. However, the complete calculation of all equipment and equipment components takes into account all interfaces for noise protection, heat protection, and fire protection. These include, for example:

— cable cross-section calculation
— creation of the system performance levels, call-by-call, fire alarm, public address system, antenna installation
— transmission networks
— design of the central devices

DIMENSIONING

All measurements are based on the above-mentioned calculations. On this basis, central devices such as antennas, fire alarm centers (BMZ), electroacoustic systems (ELA), data distributors, etc., are dimensioned and the cables are designed with corresponding structural systems.

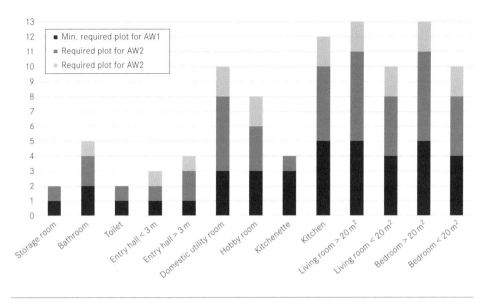

Fig. 50: Number of sockets for equipment values 1-2-3 (according to RAL-RG 678)

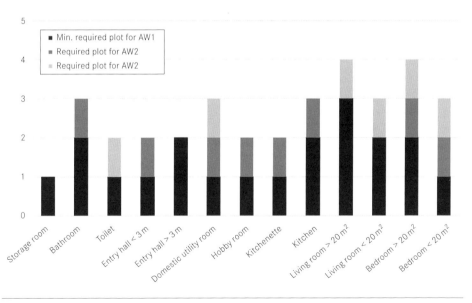

Fig. 51: Number of lighting connections for equipment values 1-2-3 (according to RAL-RG 678)

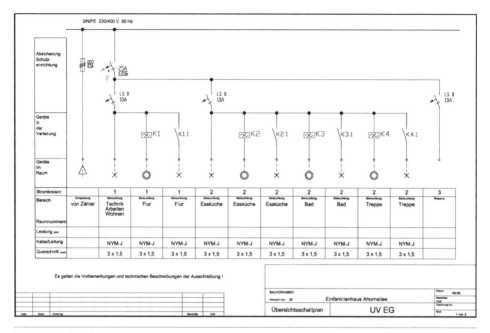

Absicherung Schutz-einrichtung		25A 0,03A F										
		LS B 10A		LS B 10A							LS B 10A	
Geräte in der Verteilung		⊗K1	K1.1	⊗K2	K2.1	⊗K3	K3.1	⊗K4	K4.1			
Geräte im Raum	△	×	◎	×	×	◎	×	◎	×	◎	×	
Stromkreisnr.		1	1	1	2	2	2	2	2	2	2	3
Bereich	Einspeisung von Zähler	Beleuchtung Technik Arbeiten Wohnen	Beleuchtung Flur	Beleuchtung Flur	Beleuchtung Essküche	Beleuchtung Essküche	Beleuchtung Essküche	Beleuchtung Bad	Beleuchtung Bad	Beleuchtung Treppe	Beleuchtung Treppe	Reserve
Raumnummern												
Leistung (W)												
Kabel/Leitung		NYM-J	NYM-J	NYM-J	NYM-J	NYM-J	NYM-J	NYM-J	NYM-J	NYM-J	NYM-J	
Querschnitt (mm²)		3 x 1,5	3 x 1,5	3 x 1,5	3 x 1,5	3 x 1,5	3 x 1,5	3 x 1,5	3 x 1,5	3 x 1,5	3 x 1,5	

Es gelten die Vorbemerkungen und technischen Beschreibungen der Ausschreibung !

BAUVORHABEN:		Datum 09.08.
PROJEKT-NR.: 20	Einfamilienhaus Ahornallee	Bearbeitet CAB
Übersichtsschaltplan	UV EG	Zeichnungs-Nr.:
		Blatt 1 von 3

Fig. 52: Overview diagram for a single-family house

DIAGRAMS

Diagrams must be drawn up that indicate additional performance data, dimensions, functions, and components, including the building automation components required to create the data. These include:

— overview diagrams for all electrical equipment > Fig. 52
— system diagrams
— function flow diagrams or descriptions for each system with function components and the principle of distribution
— power consumption lists of the electrical components provided

PLANS AND SECTIONS

A graphic representation by means of sections or enlarged details of the plans is required so that the various trades can be coordinated. These include, in particular, the laying of cables and wires, as well as their intersections.

A symbolic representation of the components (loudspeakers, fire detectors, station antenna, panels, data connections, etc.) is made in the drawings. However, for example, central units are shown in a standardized manner in order to plan the occupancy of house connections. In doing so, ground plans are created to a scale of 1:50, sections and details to a scale of between 1:50 and 1:1.

INSTALLATION DESCRIPTION

Finally, a description of the equipment components and other fixtures is provided. The performance values and specifications and, if necessary, the chosen manufacturer must be clearly documented.

In Conclusion

Nowadays, electrical planning is no longer a peripheral aspect of the planning of buildings, carried out by appointed trade companies, as was the case a decade ago. With the increasing complexity of our buildings due to increasing energy standards and expanding building maintenance requirements, buildings have become highly networked and digitally controlled. The logging of climatic data, the monitoring and control of previously manually operated components, such as windows and heating systems, the generally high degree of automation, and extensive safety and hazard monitoring ensure that cable lengths and the number of components per building have increased exponentially. Completely networked building concepts, such as Smart Home, which integrates all devices not connected to the building, including household appliances, into integral planning, show that this development will continue.

Thus, an integrated electrical planning approach is essential in order to take these issues into account from the outset. For practicing architects, it is imperative to understand the structures and principles of electrical planning and to integrate the systems. *Basics Electro-Planning* provides a clear overview of the fundamental aspects, enabling architects and engineers to coordinate and update their knowledge of electrical planning.

Appendix

STANDARDS

In order to minimize technical risks and to protect all parties involved in the handling of electrical components, in most countries electrical installations are standardized by extensive planning rules. While standards were mainly developed on a national level decades ago, initiatives are now being implemented centrally through the International Electrotechnical Commission (IEC) and subsequently transferred from regional to national standardization.

It is only if the IEC is not interested in processing a standard or if there is a time restriction that a draft design is processed regionally. If necessary, specific requirements of the building and plant operator (such as factory regulations) and the responsible distribution system operator (VNB) must also be observed and adhered to in the planning and construction of buildings.

An overview of the most important standards and standardization institutions is listed below in Tab. 10.

Tab. 10: Overview of standards and standardization institutions

Regional	America	Europe	Australasia	Asia	Africa
	PAS	CENELEC			
National	USA: ANSI	D: DIN VDE	AUS: SA	CN: SAC	SA: SABS
	CA: SCC	I: CEI	NZ: SNZ	IND: BIS	
	BR: COBEI	F: UTE	...	J: JISC	
	...	GB: BS		...	
		...			

ANSI	American National Standards Institute	JISC	Japanese Industrial Standards Committee
BIS	Bureau of Indian Standards		
BS	British Standards	PAS	Pacific Area Standards
CEI	Comitato Elettrotecnico Italiano	SA	Standards Australia
CENELEC	European Committee for Electrotechnical Standardization (fr: Comité Européen de Normalisation Electrotechnique)	SABS	South African Bureau of Standards
		SAC	Standardization Administration of China
COBEI	Comitê Brasileiro de Eletricidade, Eletrônica, Iluminação e Telecomunicações	SCC	Standards Council of Canada
		SNZ	Standards New Zealand
DIN VDE	Deutsche Industrie Norm Verband deutscher Elektrotechniker	UTE	Union Technique de l'Electricité et de la Communication
EN	European Norm		
IEC	International Electrotechnical Commission		

LITERATURE

Bert Bielefeld: *Planning Architecture*, Birkhäuser, Basel 2016

Dirk Bohne: *Technischer Ausbau von Gebäuden*, Springer Vieweg, Wiesbaden 2014

Wolfgang Burmeister, André Croissant, and Matthias Kraner: *Das Baustellenhandbuch der Elektroinstallation*, Forum, Mering 2011

Andrea Deplazes: *Constructing Architecture*, Birkhäuser, 3rd expanded edition, Basel 2013

Georg Giebeler: *Refurbishment Manual*, Birkhäuser, Basel 2009

Gerhard Hausladen: *Interiors Construction Manual*, Birkhäuser, Basel 2010

Ismail Kasikci: *Elektrotechnik für Architekten, Bauingenieure und Gebäudetechniker. Grundlagen und Anwendung in der Gebäudeplanung*, Springer Vieweg, Wiesbaden 2013

Jörn Krimmling (ed.), Uwe Deutschmann, André Preuß, and Eberhard Renner: *Atlas Gebäudetechnik. Grundlagen, Konstruktionen, Details*, 2. Auflage, Rudolf Müller, Cologne 2014

Thomas Laasch and Erhard Laasch: *Haustechnik. Grundlagen-Planung-Ausführung*, 13. Auflage, Springer Vieweg, Wiesbaden 2015

RWE: *Bau-Handbuch*, 15. Ausgabe, EW Medien und Kongresse, Essen 2014

PICTURE CREDITS
Figs. 9, 11, 12: Bert Bielefeld: Planning Architecture, Birkhauser,
    Basel 2016
Fig. 33: Busch-Jager Elektro, GmbH: Produktkatalog, Ludenscheid 2016
All other illustrations: the author

THE AUTHOR
Prof. Dr. (ETH) Peter Wotschke teaches at the Berlin School of Economics and Law and is the Chairman of the Management Board of BMC Baumanagement & Controlling AG Berlin.

Series editor: Bert Bielefeld
Concept: Bert Bielefeld, Annette Gref
Translation from German into English: Anna Roos
English copy editing: John Sweet
Project management: Silke Martini, Lisa Schulze
Layout, cover design and typography: Andreas
Hidber
Typesetting: Sven Schrape
Production: Heike Strempel

Library of Congress Cataloging-in-Publication
data
A CIP catalog record for this book has been
applied for at the Library of Congress.

Bibliographic information published by the German National Library
The German National Library lists this publication in the Deutsche Nationalbibliografie; detailed bibliographic data are available on the Internet at http://dnb.dnb.de.

This publication is also available as an e-book
(ISBN PDF 978-3-0356-1291-2;
ISBN EPUB 978-3-0356-1310-0)
and in a German language edition
(ISBN 978-3-0356-0931-8).

© 2017 Birkhäuser Verlag GmbH, Basel
P.O. Box 44, 4009 Basel, Switzerland
Part of Walter de Gruyter GmbH, Berlin/Boston

Printed on acid-free paper produced from
chlorine-free pulp. TCF ∞

Printed in Germany

ISBN 978-3-0356-0932-5

9 8 7 6 5 4 3 2 1
www.birkhauser.com